Written by: Dana Arrata

Illustrated by: Nafisa Arshad

For children ages 3- 8

ISBN 978-1-7777896-2-6

Text and illustrations copyright © 2023 by Dana Arrata

All Rights Reserved.

No part of this publication may be reproduced, stored in a retrieval system or transmitted in any form or in any means – by electronic, mechanical, photocopying, recording or otherwise – without prior written permission by the author.

GoldenPeak Communications Inc.

DISCOVER ABU DHABI with HANI & ALEEM

Abu Dhabi, UAE

Hani, a curious camel living in the desert, and his wise falcon friend Aleem were on their way to Abu Dhabi to see its famous sites. They could see a big, dusty cloud in the distance as they walked toward the city.

"It looks like a sandstorm is coming," said Aleem. "We should start the tour now before it hits."

"Okay," said Hani.

Hani was excited. He had never been to Abu Dhabi before. He couldn't wait to explore.

"Abu Dhabi is the capital city of the United Arab Emirates," explained Aleem. "There are about 2.65 million people who live here. Let's go to the Sheikh Zayed Grand Mosque first."

Suddenly, a strong gust of wind blew by them. The sand on the ground swirled in the air. The sandstorm started.

"It will be harder to see now," said Aleem. "Sandstorms make the air hazy with dust. I'll fly ahead to find the mosque. Just follow this road."

"Okay. Be careful! I don't want you to get hurt in this bad weather," Hani said. "Are you sure it's safe to fly?"

"Don't worry, I'll be fine," said Aleem.

Aleem flew away as Hani walked along the road. The blowing sand made it hard to see, but he kept going.

Finally, Hani saw a big building in the distance. It must be the Grand Mosque.

Hani could see the Grand Mosque now but couldn't see Aleem.

"Aleem!" Hani called. "Where are you?"

"Over here!" shouted Aleem.

Can you spot Aleem?

As they walked closer to the mosque, Aleem shared a few interesting facts.

"It took over 20 years to build this mosque," said Aleem. "It's the biggest mosque in the United Arab Emirates and can hold 40,000 worshippers at once."

"Wow," squealed Hani as they peered through a door to look inside. "It's beautiful."

The Grand Mosque has some of the biggest and most beautiful chandeliers in the whole world. They sparkle and shine, making the mosque look magical, especially at night.

It's a special place where people from all over the world come to pray and learn about Islam. Anyone can visit and learn about this beautiful place even if you're not Muslim.

They left the mosque and headed to Emirates Park Zoo.

"The zoo is at the end of this road," said Aleem. "It's so hard to see. I'll fly ahead to find our way. Just keep following this road until you get there."

"Okay, be careful," said Hani.

Hani continued walking and finally saw the entrance to the zoo, but he couldn't see Aleem.

"Aleem!" called Hani. "Where are you?"

"Over here!" yelled Aleem.

Can you spot Aleem?

"Let's go see the animals," said Aleem. "They have rare white tigers, elephants, giraffes, monkeys, plus a sea lion enclosure."

"I want to see the white tiger!" shouted Hani.

They were at the tiger cage and saw a white Bengal tiger playing with a big red ball.

"Why is the tiger white?" Hani asked.

Aleem explained, "White tigers are special because they are missing a pigment that gives normal Bengal tigers their orange fur, making it hard for white tigers to hide in the wild. So, they stay safe and happy in zoos where people care for them."

The tiger roared suddenly, scaring them.

"Let's get out of here!" shrieked Aleem.

They were off to Yas Island.

"Yas Island is a man-made island," explained Aleem. "There are three areas we can visit. Ferrari World has the fastest rollercoaster in the world, called Formula Rossa. Yas Waterworld is a massive water park with over 40 rides and slides. And Yas Marina Circuit, is a huge racetrack that hosts Formula One races."

"I'll fly ahead to see if it's open today. Just keep following this road."

"Okay, be careful," called Hani.

Hani kept walking and saw a huge roller coaster in the distance.

"This must be Yas Island," he said to himself, but he couldn't see Aleem.

"Aleem!" called Hani. "Where are you?"

"Up here!" yelled Aleem.

Can you spot Aleem?

Hani waited for Aleem to get off the rollercoaster.

Suddenly, he heard a call for help. "Aleem, where are you?" hollered Hani. There was no answer. He yelled again, "Aleem, where are you?"

He heard a faint moan. "Over here," cried Aleem.

Hani found Aleem standing on the ground, looking sad and confused.

"What happened?" asked Hani. "Are you okay?"

"A big gust of wind blew me away," replied Aleem. "I couldn't see where I was going. I flew into something hard and fell to the ground. I think I broke my wing."

"Oh no!" squealed Hani. "We need to find help."

"It's okay," said Aleem. "I know where to go. You'll have to give me a ride on your hump because I don't think I can fly."

"We need to go to the Abu Dhabi Falcon Hospital," said Aleem. "The hospital is at the end of this road."

The wind blew, and the air was thick with sand. They could see the outline of a building ahead.

"There it is. Do you see it? There's a falcon statue in front of the hospital," said Aleem.

"I think so," Hani replied.

Can you spot the falcon statue?

They went inside and waited in the waiting room for a doctor to see Aleem.

"This is a veterinary hospital for sick and injured falcons," explained Aleem. "It's the largest falcon hospital in the world. Over 11,000 falcons visit yearly for checkups and treatment. They also take care of other kinds of birds and animals. A doctor can help me here."

"Great – it sounds like you're in good hands," Hani replied with a sigh of relief.

It was Aleem's turn to see the doctor. They went into a room where the doctor examined his wing.

"I think it's broken," said the doctor, "but we need to take an X-ray to know for sure."

Aleem had never had an X-ray before.

"I'm scared," said Aleem.

"Don't worry," said the doctor. "We're going to take a picture of your wing with a special camera. The X-ray will show us your bones to see if any are broken. It's really easy, and it won't hurt at all."

"It's okay," said Hani. "I'm here with you, so you don't have to be scared."

Aleem took a deep breath and tried to relax as they X-rayed his wing.

The X-ray showed one broken bone in Aleem's wing.

The doctor bandaged his wing so the bone would stay in place and heal, and he said to rest and return to the hospital in two weeks for a check-up.

"I'm so glad you're alright," Hani said. "Sandstorms are dangerous when you can't see where you're going."

"You're right," said Aleem. "I've learned my lesson. I won't fly around a big city during a sandstorm ever again. I'll have to stay close to home for a while because I can't fly right now."

"Don't worry, my friend," Hani reassured. "I'm here to help you with whatever you need."

"Thanks," said Aleem. "Let's go home."

Aleem sat on Hani's hump as they walked through the desert. The wind was blowing, but the worst of the sandstorm was over.

"We're almost there," said Aleem. "I think I see my nest."

"Yes, I see it," said Hani.

He could see the big tree and Aleem's nest in the distance.

Can you spot the nest?

Aleem hopped from Hani's hump into his nest.

"Thanks for taking me around Abu Dhabi today," said Hani. "I'm so sorry you broke your wing."

"I had fun showing you the sights," replied Aleem. "Thank you for being there for me when I got hurt."

"That's what friends are for," said Hani.

Aleem sighed with relief, knowing he could always count on his good friend.

"Don't worry. I'll stay and help you for the next two weeks and take you back to see the doctor," Hani said with a caring smile.

"Thank you," chirped Aleem. "I'm so grateful to have you as my friend."